HOW DO WE

LOCAL DIRECTORIES

BILL BOYLE

GENERAL EDITOR: DAVID PENROSE

COLLINS EDUCATIONAL

INTRODUCTION

Historical study depends upon an ability to analyse, interpret and use evidence about the past.

The evidence, in this case, is documentary, specifically, local Directories. Some of these appeared as early as the eighteenth century, but they became a rich source of local history as their numbers increased in the nineteenth century. Initially commercial directories for business contacts, their purpose evolved to providing exact information for Post Office deliveries, and subsequently detailing the occupations of an area's householders.

Throughout the book, the reader follows one child's exploration of his local directories as he builds up a picture of the history of his town. The role of the local librarian in providing and interpreting material is emphasised, and children are encouraged to investigate the past through the evidence supplied in their local directories.

Bill Boyle is Deputy Headteacher of Manor Junior School in Birkenhead. He is the author of several educational books and has many years teaching experience.

© 1987 Bill Boyle

First published in Great Britain 1987 by
Collins Educational
8 Grafton Street, London W1X 3LA

Typeset by V&M Graphics Ltd, Aylesbury, Bucks
Printed in Great Britain by Butler & Tanner Ltd, Somerset

ISBN 0 00 315413 0

All rights reserved. No part of this publication may be reproduced, stored in a retrieval system, or transmitted, in any form or by any means, electronic, mechanical, photocopying, recording or otherwise, without the prior permission of the publishers.

CONTENTS

Why Directories? 5

Looking at a village 8

Local traditions 16

Transport — sea and land 22

Changing trades 30

Changing times 33

Local industry 37

History of a street 41

How to do it yourself 47

Index 48

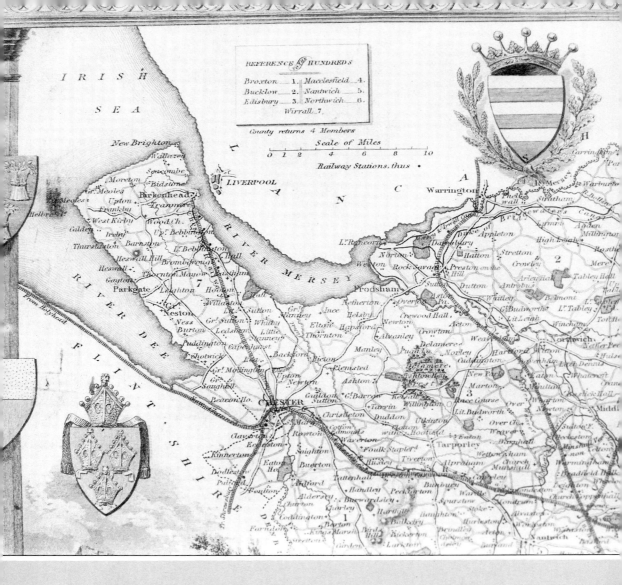

Maps showing the position of Neston — the village which appears in this book

Why Directories?

In this book we are going to show you how *local Directories* can be useful sources of information about your particular town or village by following the research of John into his home village of Neston in Cheshire.

You all probably know what a *modern* business directory looks like. They are known as the Yellow Pages. Here is a section from it. As in early Directories, local tradespeople buy space on the page to advertise their business.

◆**Leathergoods shops**
SEE ALSO SUEDE GOODS RETAILERS: TRAVEL GOODS

A Touch of Leather Ltd, 41 Kensington High St, W8....01-**937** 6054
Alami Import & Export Ltd, 19 Kingsland Rd, E2........01-**729** 5501
Azezio Fashion Ltd, 394 Edgware Rd, W2................01-**723** 3878
Benni Ltd, 12 William St, SW1..........................01-**245** 9672
Brandbest Ltd,
 163 Stoke Newington Church St, N16....01-**249** 0725
Bucci, 16 Princes Arc Jermyn St, SW1..................01-**734** 1846
Cactus Leather, 220 Grafton Rd, NW5...................01-**267** 2289
Celine of Paris—
 28 New Bond St, W1 ....01-**493** 9000
City Bag Store The—
 7 Shopping Arc Kensington High St, W8.............01-**938** 2463
 434 Strand, WC2 ....01-**379** 7762
Coram Shop, 56 Coram St, WC1 ....01-**278** 1231
Curio 2 Co Ltd, 287 Oxford St, W1 ....01-**491** 3577
Dario Leather Clothing,
 114 Kensington Mkt Kensington High St, W8....01-**937** 5160
Dolomite, 116 Queensway, W2...........................01-**229** 5686
Eagle Accessories, 262 Oxford St, W1 ....01-**493** 4727
Etienne Aigner Ltd, 6 New Bond St, W1.................01-**491** 7764
                                                   TX 21356
Fior Ltd—
 27 Brompton Rd, SW3...............................01-**589** 0053
Gladstone, 47 Aldwych, WC2............................01-**240** 0494
Gold Pfeil, 107 Jermyn St, SW1 ....01-**839** 3315
Gucci Ltd, 27 Old Bond St, W1 ....01-**629** 2716
                                                   TX 21406
Guisseppe Leather & Electrical Goods,
 134 Gray's Inn Rd, WC1...01-**278** 6639
Harborow's, 41 Burlington Arc, W1.....................01-**493** 8939
Henry's—
 185 Brompton Rd, SW3..............................01-**589** 2011
 Do..01-**589** 7119
 201 Regent St, W1.................................01-**437** 6542
 Do..01-**437** 6579
Hermes Ltd—
 3 Royal Exch, EC3.................................01-**626** 7794
Houghton & Co (London) Ltd, 37 Poultry, EC2...........01-**600** 0722
Hughes K.J, 26 Ponsonby Pl, SW1.......................01-**821** 6443
Inca Leather Fashions, 97 Redchurch St, E2............01-**729** 6948
Jemmini, 83 Wigmore St, W1............................01-**935** 0149
Kent Leather at Lillywhites, 24 Regent St, SW1........01-**839** 4277
Le Soir Handbags Ltd, 110 New Bond St, W1.............01-**629** 5850
Leather Goods Repairers, 14 Livonia St, W1............01-**439** 3909
Leather Machine Ltd, 163 King's Rd, SW3...............01-**352** 8965
Leather Rat—
 45 Mortimer St, W1................................01-**636** 1994
 26 Wellington St, WC2.............................01-**240** 0789
Loewe Leather Goods—
 25a Old Bond St, W1 ....01-**493** 3914
                                                   TX 298697
 47 Brompton Rd, SW3...............................01-**581** 4014
Magenta—
 5 Avery Rw, W1....................................01-**499** 4435
Mindel J. Ltd—
 136 Edgware Rd, W2................................01-**723** 5132
 Harben Pde 8 Finchley Rd, NW3.....................01-**722** 1152

Xotique,
 153 Kensington Mkt Kensington High St, W8...01-**937** 0768

◆**Legal aid & advice**
SEE CONVEYANCING CONSULTANTS: INFORMATION SERVICES: SOLICITORS

◆**Legations**
SEE EMBASSIES, CONSULATES, HIGH COMMISSIONS & LEGATIONS

◆**Leisure centres**
SEE ALSO SQUASH COURTS

Allington Court Gymnasium 1982 Ltd, Allington Court,
 Allington Street, SW1...01-**828** 3647
Blackheath Leisure (Carousel) Ltd,
 96 Elephant & Castle Shopping Centre, SE1...01-**703** 3288
Britannia Leisure Centre, 40 Hyde Rd, N1..............01-**729** 5400
Civil Service Recreation Centre, Monck St, SW1........01-**799** 7661
Covent Garden Community Centre,
 46 Earlham St, WC2...01-**240** 9720
First Leisure Corporation PLC, 7 Soho St, W1..........01-**437** 9727
 Do..01-**434** 1388
Group Five Holdings Ltd,
 11 Great Marlborough St, W1...01-**439** 3853
 Do..01-**439** 3903
Hackney, London Borough of—
 Baths & Laundries,
 Whiston Rd Baths, E2..............................01-**739** 4797
Inter-Action—
 City Fm 1, 232 Grafton Rd, NW5....................01-**485** 4585
Jubilee Hall Recreation Centre, 6 Maiden La, WC2......01-**240** 6830
 Do..01-**836** 4835
Jubilee Hall Recreation Centre, Covent Gdn, WC2.......01-**240** 6848
Kunick Holdings Plc, 92 Tooley St, SE1.................01-**378** 6096
Last Chance Centre, 87 Masbro Rd, W14.................01-**603** 7118
Mornington Sports & Leisure Centre,
 142 Arlington Rd, NW1...01-**267** 3600
St. Georges Adventure Playground, Crowder St, E1.....01-**480** 5066
Young Men's Christian Association—
 London Central,
 112 Great Russell St, WC1, CentymcA Club..........01-**637** 8131

◆**Lens mfrs**
SEE OPTICAL GOODS MFRS & WH'SALERS

5

This advertisement from a local paper shows how business people know that a new edition of the Yellow Pages is being prepared.

This advertisement is for Business Pages, another Directory. What kind of people would use Business Pages? What information would they find useful in it? How many editions of each Business Pages are there? Is there a reason for this? Which part of a Directory helps you to locate the information that you want, quickly? Make a list of as many different modern Directories as you can find. Alongside their names, write what they are used for.

As far as directories go, ours is the business.

Business Pages has been carefully designed to solve business problems,

not create them.

Which is why it's published in seven convenient geographical editions. (One for each of the major commercial/industrial centres in Britain.)

Turn to the back of the book and you'll find the index.

Turn to the front of the book and you'll also find the index. (Well, we like to keep everyone happy.)

And, in addition to our comprehensive classified listings, you'll discover an alphabetical listing of company names, addresses, and telephone numbers.

A listing, we might add, that's a little more comprehensive than most.

So look out for Business Pages. (We send a free local area copy to your company every year.) You'll find our format far more informative.

Business Pages.
A directory, not an indirectory.

Why were Directories written?

At the end of the seventeenth century, about 300 years ago, trade between towns increased. Merchants needed to know where to find businessmen in other towns, who would buy their goods. The first such *commercial* Directory was a list made in 1677 of London merchants. However, history detectives had to wait until the nineteenth century to find enough Directories printed, to make research useful.

These early Directories were published for business reasons, to make contact between buyer and seller. You could say that they were the original Yellow Pages for business people. The Directories were named after historians or commercial firms which produced the Directories.

Here is the first page of the first published Directory, dated 1789, for the Chester area. It contains 'an alphabetical list of the merchants, tradesmen, in the city.'

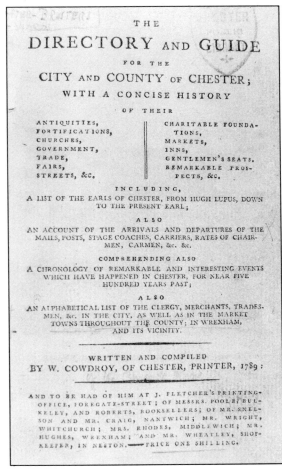

Looking at a village

The Cross, Neston

A view from The Cross, in High Street, Neston

John Ellis calls at McColls Newsagents, in the High Street, each morning on his way to school. Look for it on the photograph.

John has got to know Jim Southern, the shop manager, very well.

Mr Southern has always lived in Neston, and has told John many interesting stories about his childhood there. Mr Southern told John that he was born in Neston in 1932. At that time, his father was the town newsagent, and the family lived over his shop.

There is an old photograph of the shop hanging on the wall. Look carefully at the photograph on the next page. Can you spot the newsagent?

Can you tell what the newsagent was called? It is not called after Mr Southern's father because the photograph was taken just before Mr Southern took over the shop. How does the newsagent look different to the McColls shop in the first photograph?

What shops are on either side? A magnifying glass will help you to see what goods are being displayed in their windows.

Notice the shop with the name Hancock. What can you see on either side of the name? These give a clue to the goods sold in the shop.

Compare the two photographs. They show the same block of shops. List any other differences you can see between the two photographs.

Try to think of reasons why these changes have happened.

What things have *not* changed?

Look closely at the plaque up on the wall. Why do you think this part of Neston High Street is given this name?

Digging deeper

John Ellis wanted to find out more information about the history of Jim Southern's shop.

He decided to visit the local library. There, the librarian helped John look through the local history files in the reference section of the library.

While searching through these, John came across a book printed in 1935. It was called *Cope's Cheshire Directory and Buyer's Guide*. In the section about Neston, he found:

CONFECTIONERS
Anyon H, 3 Raby road
Atkinson J M, The Cross
Bushell M, Liverpool road
Fewtrell W, 12 Station road, Parkgate
Hale A G, Parkgate road
Ledsham F W Parade, Parkgate
Mealor A, Station rd, Parkgate
Reid F S, Bridge street
Roberts G, Mill st
Tansey G, Cheltenham Walk, near Parkgate Station

CYCLE DEALERS & REPRS.
Cameron M G, The Cross
CHRIMES J, Brook Street Yard

DAIRY FARMERS
Nicholls W K, Ashfield Farm, The Cross & 1 Brook st. Tel 211 & 286 Neston

DAIRYKEEPERS
Sisson W, High street

DRAPERS
Nicholson F W, High st,
Oakes & Griffiths, Parkgate road

ENGINEERS (Agricultural)
Bridson R & Sons, Park Vale

ENGINEERS (Electrical)
Reid Arthur, High street. Tel Neston 164

FANCY GOODS DEALERS
Baddeley R, Chester road
SOUTHERN H, The Cross. Phone 317
Tranter C, Parkgate road

FISH CATERERS
Jones W D, Liverpool road
Smith J, High st

FISHMONGERS
Dee Shellfish Co, Parkgate

FRUITERERS & GRNGCRS
Birch E, Bridge street
Davidson M, Ness Village

Gallimore J, The Cross
Hare J G, High st
Mealer S, High st
Weston M, Park street. Tel 309

FURNITURE DEALERS
Watson G, Parkgate road

GENERAL DEALERS
Howe W P, The Stores, Parade, Parkgate; also confectioner

GROCERS
Cannon M, Little Neston
Castle I, High street
Chester Co-operative Society, High st
Evans W, Liverpool rd. Phone 132 Neston
Ewbank A O, Two Mills
Hughes J R, High st
Irwin J Sons & Co Ltd, The Cross
Lythgoe's, Little Neston
PEARSON'S, Bridge street. Tel 110 Neston
Prosser H. Parkgate
Rees J, The Cross
The Stores (Edwards J A), Ness Village
Wilde J, Nese Village

HAIRDRESSERS
Beattle R W Park street
Corkhill J, High street
Fairclough H, High st

HAULAGE CONTRACTORS
Gray D G W, Leighton rd. Tel

HOTELS & PUBLIC HOUSES
Brewers Arms, Park st,
Brown Horse Inn, The Cross,
Chester Hotel, Parkgate;
Coach & Horses, Bridge st. A Marr, proprietor
Greenland Fishery, Parkgate road
Holywell Hotel, Parkgate
Malt Shovel, Liverpool road, Neston, Propr John Wheeler
Neston Hotel, High st
Red Lion, Parkgate
Royal Oak, Little Neston;
The Wheat Sheaf Inn, Ness,

Union Hotel, Parkgate
White Horse, The Cross

IRONMONGERS
Appleton J A T, High st

LADIES' AND CHILDREN'S HAIRDRESSER
'Brynmor,' High street; propr, E F Jones. Tel 281 Neston

LAUNDRIES
Neston & Parkgate Laundry Co Ltd

MOTOR BODY BUILDERS
TWO MILLS ENGINEERING CO., Welsh Cross Roads, Ladsham. Tel Hooton 24. And Little Sutton. Tel Hooton 119

MOTOR ENGINEERS AND GARAGES
Cameron M C The Cross all accessessories stocked; expert repairs.
CHRIMES J, Brook street yard Gilmore Bros, Leighton
HILL R G, Chester road. Tel 70
Howard T H, Chester High rd, Burton
LEEMAN'S GARAGE (Propr, R T Leeman), Parade, Parkgate. Appointed A.A. Garage. Phone Neston No 82
TWO MILLS ENGINEERING CO, Welsh Cross Roads, Ledsham. Phone Hooton 24. And Little Sutton. Tel Hooton 119
Meltcalfe, G. High st
Mostyns Garage, Parkgate
Williams & Bell, High street

NEWSAGENTS
Howe W P, The Stores, Parade, Parkgate
SOUTHERN H, The Cross. Phone 317

NURSERYMEN & FLORISTS
Jamieson A, Floral Nursery, Church lane

PAINTERS & PLUMBERS
Anyon H, 3 Raby road
Coventry W M, Mill st
Hough W A., High street. Phone 118
Johnson's, High st. Phone 64

John looked eagerly at the section headed Newsagents. Did he find what he was looking for? Read through the Directory entries, and you will find out what else H. Southern sold in 1935.

What did the newsagent have, that only a few of the other shops listed, had in 1935? (Clue: We need to have a special kind of Directory for this today!)

What evidence can you find on this page of *Cope's Directory* that suggests a picture of life in Neston in 1935? Notice the type of work that people did in the area.

Pictorial evidence

Looking at this page, John recognised the names of some buildings that he sees in Neston today. They are still in use as hotels or public houses.

The buildings were all listed in the section for Hotels and Public houses, in the Directory. John was puzzled when he spotted the name White Horse, The Cross, in this section. The White Horse building is still there today, but it is no longer a hotel.

John found this photograph in a local history book. It is pictorial evidence to prove that the written entry in the Directory is correct.

Look carefully at the photograph. Identify two other buildings which are listed in the Directory. Which section are they in?

Why do you think that Grisdale's cafe (shown on the photograph) is not listed on the pages we have reproduced from the Directory?

Reading a Directory

Kelly's Cheshire Directory of 1939 gave John a further piece of information about Harry Southern. What was it? What does this suggest to you about Southern's business?

Pritchard Jessie (Mrs.), newsagt. High st TN 490
Redfern Danl. fruit, High st. T N 484
Roberts C. W. Ltd. coal & coke mers. High st. T N 294
Robinson Robin, cycle dlr. Chester rd
Royal Oak P.H. (Jas. Carroll), Little Neston
Scarratt Lily (Miss), shopkpr. The Cross
Scott Arth. hay & straw dlr. Bridge st. T N 355
Scott Rt. farmer, Ivy farm, Little Neston
Selby Robert M.B., Ch.B., F.R.C.S. physician & surgeon (firm, Carlisle, Gunn, Selby & Turner), Parkgate road. T N 58
Shiber Chas, refrshmnt. rms. Hawthorne cott. Parkgate rd
Shrewsbury Arms P.H. (Percy Butterworth), Hinderton rd. T N 58
Simpson Alex. M.B., Ch.B. physcn. & surgn. Parkgate rd. T N 466
Sisson Wm. farmer, Uplands, Upper Raby rd
Smith Jsph, fried fish dlr. High st
Southern Harry, newsagt. The Cross & Bridge st. T N 317
Watson George, cabinet maker, Parkgate road
Weston Margt. (Miss), greengro. Park st. T N 309
Williams Chas. motor car propr. High st. T N 147

Make a list of the people, and their occupations, who appear in *both* the *Kelly* and *Cope Directory* pages.

Are there any other newsagents listed since the 1935 Directory?

Using the 1939 Directory, list the jobs which you would not find being done in a town today. Some of the jobs listed are still being done, but they have different names, for example, Smith Jsph.fried fish dlr...

What would a 'fried fish dealer' be called today? Can you find any others?

Look at the two Directories. How are they set out differently?

Set out the information from the *Kelly Directory* under group headings.

John found the *Kelly Directory* very interesting. It gave lots of information about Neston. Here is an extract from the introduction.

> NESTON-CUM-PARKGATE is a parish, formed by Local Government Board Order No. 31,631, Sept. 30, 1894, from the former townships of Great Neston, Little Neston and Leighton, and is governed by an Urban District Council. The "Local Government Act, 1858", was adopted by Great Neston and Parkgate July 2, 1867, and the district governed by a Local Board, but under the provisions of the Local Government Act, 1894, an Urban District Council was established. By the County of Chester Review Order, 1933, part of this parish was added to the parish of Raby, and the township of Ness added to this parish. By the same Order a new Urban District was formed, to be known as the Neston Urban District, consisting of 5 wards, with 17 members. Gas and electricity are available. Neston and Parkgate parish has its own water resources. The parishes of Willaston, Burton and Ness in this Urban District are supplied with water by the West Cheshire Water Board. The area of Neston-cum-Parkgate civil parish is 3,285 acres; the population in 1931 was 5,690. The area of Neston Urban District is 8,495 acres of land and inland water; the population in 1931 was 7,911.
>
> The population of the wards in 1931 was:—Burton and Ness, 961; Leighton and Parkgate, 1,813; Little Neston, 1,633; Neston, 2,244; Willaston 1,260.

From the Directory, John noticed that, in 1933, the Neston Urban District was formed. It was made up of five wards. Make a list of them and their populations.

John started to draw a graph, showing the populations of the five wards. Use the information on your list to finish John's graph.

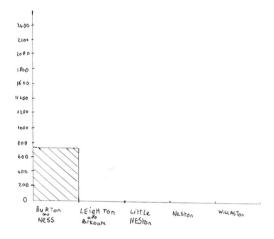

John drew this map to show the position of Neston on the Wirral. He then divided Neston into its five wards.

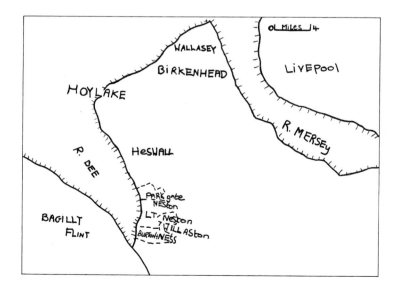

What other information about Neston can you find in the passage?

14

You can see from the *Cope's Directory* that Trades people are *classified* (listed) under general headings. How are these headings printed so that the reader can quickly find the business or service that they want?

Can you find which of the businesses listed in the *Cope's Directory*, page 10, might help these people?

'Who can help me?'

Where could she get help?

Who will sell today's catch for them?

'Where can I get a spare wheel?'

These early commercial Directories were paid for by the local tradesmen who advertised their business in them.

Local traditions

Neston market

During the school holiday, John takes his grandmother around the market, which is held every Friday. He was surprised when she told him that there had always been a market in Neston – as far back as her own grandmother could remember.

His curiosity aroused by this, John decided to see how far back he could trace Neston's market.

Several of the local Directories mentioned it. It was already there in 1789 as *Cowdroy's Directory and Guide* records that Neston is a place 'where is a good market on Friday'. *Pigot's Cheshire Directory*, 1828–9, notes briefly that 'market day is Friday'. While *Robson's Commercial Directory* of 1841 describes Neston as 'a market town in the hundred of Wirral'.

John also found that the site for the town market had changed over the years. It used to be held in the High Street, but now it is behind the Town Hall. Why do you think the market site changed? (Clue: look at the photograph on page 8.)

John made a list of the goods being sold at the market today. Copy his list and tick the items that you think could have been on sale in an 1840's market. Put a cross by the things which would *definitely* not have been, and give your reasons.

John's market list

- Fruit
- Vegetables
- Meat
- Fish
- Shoes
- bed linen
- Clothes
- electrical goods
- antiques
- Pots and pans
- Plants
- records and tapes
- Carpet
- Wool
- Sports kit
- Cakes
- Jewellery
- microwave ovens

The librarian helped John to find out how the market started in Neston. They discovered that a Royal Charter had been granted by King George II in 1728, for a market to be held each Friday at The Cross.

Here is part of the original copy of the Royal Charter. It is written in Latin. Below is a translation of it into English.

> GEORGE THE SECOND, BY THE GRACE OF GOD, King of Great Britain, France and Ireland, Defender of the Faith, etc, to ALL to whom our present letters shall come, greetings.
>
> … it was discovered that it would not be to the damage or prejudice of ourselves or of others nor would it be harmful to neighbouring markets and fairs if we should grant to Roger Mostyn, Baronet … and to his heirs, licence to have and to hold within the manor of Great Neston in the Hundred of Wirral in the County of Chester aforesaid one market on Friday each week for ever and three annual fairs every year … for the the buying and selling of all and every kind of horses and cattle, flesh, fish, birds, grain, roots, herbs and other provisions and each and every kind of marketable goods and merchandise commonly bought and sold in markets and fairs.

Since Sir Roger Mostyn was granted the Charter in 1728, Neston has held its weekly Friday market. However, John discovered, by searching through the local Directories, that it was discontinued for some years during the 1850 s, when the town was hit by hard times.

John found evidence of this in *Francis White's History, Gazeteer and Directory of Cheshire*. This was published in 1860, and stated that 'the market which was held on Friday is now obsolete [no more].' The hard times couldn't have lasted too long, because *Kelly's Cheshire Directory* of 1892 confirms that once again 'the market day is Friday'.

Does your town have a market? How often is it held? Is it always on the same day? Local street names often give clues to the sites of old markets. Ask your local librarian to help you find out how long your market has been held.

The Neston Fair

John enjoys going to the fair. It is held in Neston once a year, in the market place.

He showed his grandmother this photograph of the fair. She said that she remembered her mother talking about the Neston Donkey Fair.

This old photograph shows the donkeys and their owners gathered at The Cross. The 'donkey fairs' were held between 1887 and 1891, supported by the Society for the Prevention of Cruelty to Animals (later became the RSPCA).

John found from information in these local Directories that Neston had another type of Fair. What was it? How often was it held each year? When did it stop?

> The fairs are held on February 2nd, May 29th, and September 29th, for cattle.
> *Robson's Commercial Directory*, 1841.
>
> These are fairs on February 2nd, May 29th, and September 29th, for cattle.
> *Kelly's Cheshire Directory*, 1857.
>
> The cattle fairs, formerly held on February 2nd, May 29th and September 29th, are now discontinued.
> *Kelly's Cheshire Directory*, 1892.

Using the picture and directory clues, write a description of 'Neston Fair—Yesterday and Today'. Draw a scene from the fair, old or modern, to illustrate your writing. Do you have a fair in your town? See what evidence you can find about its history.

Neston Ladies Day

Each year, John receives a welcome extra day's holiday from school on the first Thursday in June. This is the day of the anniversary walk of the Neston Female Friendly Society – so all the local schools are closed!

The reason for this annual holiday was explained at school. John learnt that the Society was the idea of the local vicar, Thomas Ward, in 1814, to raise 'a fund by voluntary subscription, towards the support of the old, sick, lame and infirm members'.

In *Cowdroy's Directory of Chester*, 1789, John found that Thomas Ward was the vicar then. Who was his curate?

John searched through *Pigot's Directory* of 1822, but could find no mention of the Rev. Ward. So he had obviously left Neston, soon after the founding of the Friendly Society.

> *Neston Directory*
> Neston,
>
> Rev. Tho. Ward, vicar
> Rev. Rich. Carter, curate
> John Glegg, efq.
> Charles Lewis, efq.
> William Johnson, gent.
> Samuel Ellaby, gent.
> Thomas Forthall, gent.
> John Williams, gent.
> —Gregory, gent.
> Thomas Woods, attorney
> Edw. Humphreys, ditto
> Edmund Lyon, beer-brewer
> John Watmough, ditto
> Mr. Wolfenholme, apothecary
> Mr. Turner, ditto
> Mr. Harrison, ditto

Neston Female Friendly Society in the 1910s

What was a Friendly Society? These Societies had existed long before 1814, but the Neston Society was the first of its kind. Can you guess why it was different?

Find out if there was ever a Friendly Society in your town.

What was its purpose? Does it still exist? What was its title?

Does it have an annual celebration or anniversary?

Why do you think most of the Friendly Societies disappeared during the twentieth century?

Transport—sea and land

Parkgate seafront

Every Saturday morning, John walks down to nearby Parkgate seafront to buy fish for his grandmother. He always goes to Mealor's shop.

Parkgate seafront. Do you notice the grass?

The Mealors are the only fishing family left in Parkgate. John has seen references to the Mealors as fishermen in an earlier local Directory.

Fishermen unloading their catch in the 1930s

List the names and addresses of any fishermen named in this extract from the *Kelly's Cheshire Directory* of 1939. Why is there only one family still fishing at Parkgate today? Clue: Examine the top photograph on the opposite page carefully.

Crook Vincent M. chemist, & post office, The Parade. Neston 133
Cross Jn. Hy. fisherman
Feutrell Wm. fishermen, Station rd
Gibbons E. antique dlr. The Parade
Green Shutter Café (Mrs. E. Hitchmough, proprietess)
Greenfell Algernon Marshall Daryl M.A. preparatory school, Mostyn ho. The Parade. Neston 10
Higgins Fred, fisherman, The Parade
Hollywell Temperance Hotel, The Parade. T N Neston 142
Hopes Rosamond (Miss), café, The Parade
Howe Wm. Parker, shopkpr. The Parade
Jervis Thos. coal mer. T N Neston 218
Johnson Edwd. shopkpr. 6 Station rd
Jones Ada Eliz. (Mrs.), boarding ho. Seaward ho. Parade. Neston 344
Jones Jn. Edwd. insur. agt. Cartref, Brooklands rd. Neston 513
Lane Eliz. (Mrs.), café, The Parade

Ledsham Wm. confctnr. The Parade
Leeman Thos. R. motor engnr. The Parade. T N Neston 82
Macmillan Marie (Mrs.), boarding ho. Overdee, The Parade. Neston 387
Mealor Alfd. haulage contrctr. Station rd. Neston 349
Mealor Geo. fisherman, New cott
Mealor Jn. Herbt. fisherman, Hill view, The Parade
Mealor Tom, café, The Parade
Neston & District Cricket Club (G. D Walford, sec.). Neston 199
Nicholls' Ashfield Farm Dairy, The Parade
Parkgate Products Ltd. food specialities mfrs. Neston 304
Parkgate Swimming Baths (A Canning, manager). Neston 245
Paulo Kennels (Miss Ann Paul, principal), The Parade. Neston 167
Peters Hy. fisherman, Station rd
Peters Jas. fisherman, Mostyn ter

Peters Richard, fisherman, The Parade
Prosser Joyce (Mrs.), shopkpr. The Parade. Neston 310
Red Lion P.H. (Jsph. Moore), The Parade
Richardson May (Miss), ladies' school, Leighton, Boathouse la. T N Neston 168
Rigby House Holiday Home (Mrs. Laura Davies, manageress), The Parade
Robinson Jas. coal dlr. Station yard
Smith James, fisherman, Station rd
Smith Joseph, fisherman, The Parade
Stephenson C. & R. (Misses), café, The Parade. Neston 456
Stringer Harry Martindale, boarding ho. Ivy cott. The Parade. Neston 303
Swift C. & Son, butchers, The Parade. Neston 123
Tansey Gertrude (Miss), confetnr. Station rd
Tyson & Sons, bldrs. Lancelyn, Brooklands rd

Look closely at the pages of *Kelly's Directory* to see if you can spot a popular pastime for the youngsters who came to Parkgate front in the 1930s. Sadly it has now been demolished.

This extract from *Cowdroy's Directory* of 1789 told John that Parkgate had been used by bigger ships than fishing boats.

NESTON

LIES ten miles N. W. Chester, in Wirral hundred, where is a good market on Friday. Its situation is highly favoured, the inhabitants enjoying the most desirable advantages from purity of air and pleasantness of prospects. Nor are these advantages the less, from its contiguity to Parkgate, where the convenience of sea bathing is inferior to none;—indeed, the growing attention shewn to it, during these seasons, is a better proof of its accommodation in this particular, than any recommendation that can be given of it here. Both these towns are tolerably populous; and the interest and reputation of them have of late been not a little increased by the extensive and brilliant patronage shewn to the Parkgate packets; which, from the regularity of their sailing, the excellence of their accommodations, and every other advantage, seem to have a decided ascendency over all others; and, in consequence, Parkgate is become the resort of elegance and fashion. These packets sail regularly at least four times a week. Neston contains a very good church.

Neston Directory

Neston,
Thomas Jones, skinner
Sarah Jones, ditto
Joseph Jones, butcher
Richard Longley, ditto
William Maddock; ditto
Samuel Norman, ditto
Robert Jones, butcher
James Norman, ditto
Wm. Ellis, inn-keeper, polt-office
Hornby Rowe, inn-keeper
William Coventry, fen, ditto
William Leach, ditto
John Quay, ditto
John Oliver, importer of cows from Ireland to Parkgate and Liverpool
Joseph Barrow, taylor
William Davenport, ditto
John Shakshaft, ditto
John Griffith, ditto
William Glover, bricklayer
Henry Youds, slater,
John Jones, joiner
Andrew Gibbons, ditto
John Haswell, wheelwright and carpenter
John Ralphs, ditto
Thomas Wynne, ditto
Tho Jones, tythe-collector
John Robinson, cooper
Richard Wynne, ditto
Richard Evans, black smith
Jon Brownsworth, turner
Tho. Rudd, excise-office
William Nixon, gardener
John Banks, Chester carrier
Peter Parr, ditto
Samuel Lea, Liverpool carrier

Moor-side,
Rev. Mr. Price
William Ryland, sail-maker
John Matthews, gent.
—Matthews, agent to the Parkgate packets
Little Neston
Thomas Cottingham, esq.
Ness
Joshua Small
William Davies, collier, agent to the colliery
John Humphreys, officer of customs
Willaston,
William Leghbound, miller
Joseph Mason
Raby,
Thomas Ashbrooke, gent.
Burton,
Rev. William Watts
Edward Parry
Parkgate,
Hon. T. Fitzmaurice
Thomas Massey, esq.
Edward Williams, esq.
Mr B. Monk, officer of customs
Mr. W. Monk, ditto
Mr. Spencer, George
Mr. Briscoe, Talbot
Mr. Shone, White lion
Capt. Hervey, of the King Dublin packet
Capt. Miller, Queen ditto
Capt. Heird, Prince of Wales ditto
Capt. Brown, Princess Royal ditto
Capt. Torty, Hawk,
Capt. Guile, Salisbury
Capt. Hammond, Pleasure Yacht
Mrs. Rathbone, shop-keeper

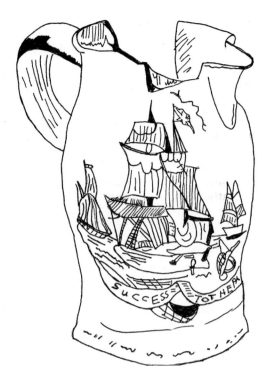

John's sketch of the Parkgate Packet Jug, which was made in the 1790s as a souvenir and shows the packet ships. It is now in the Merseyside County Museum.

In the late eighteenth century, five 'packet' boats ferried passengers between Parkgate and Dublin, Ireland.

Read the Directory extract to find out why the Parkgate 'packets' were so popular. What does the Directory listing for John Oliver tell you? How was his work linked to the 'packets'? Thomas Rudd is listed as an excise officer. What work would he do? List the sea captains who lived in Parkgate at that time. What was the occupation of the two Monk brothers? Find, from the Directory, whom you would contact to arrange to travel on the 'packets'.

White's Cheshire Directory of 1860, gave John the reason why Parkgate stopped being a busy port, and returned to the life of a sleepy, fishing village. How long did the 'packet' trade last?

> About fifty years ago Parkgate presented all the appearance of a seaport, there being at that time six packets besides other vessels constantly employed in the trade with Ireland. At the present period however this as a packet station is completely negated as vessels beyond eighty tons burthen cannot come within a considerable distance of the quay. A large sand-bank occupies the former channel.

Road and rail

While the 'packet' boats were sailing from Neston cum Parkgate to Dublin, it was necessary to have a good road for travellers to use to reach the port. In 1787, a *turnpike* road was opened to link Chester to Neston. Soon, another connected Neston to Birkenhead and the River Mersey. See *'Time and Motion'* another book in this series, for information on turnpike roads.

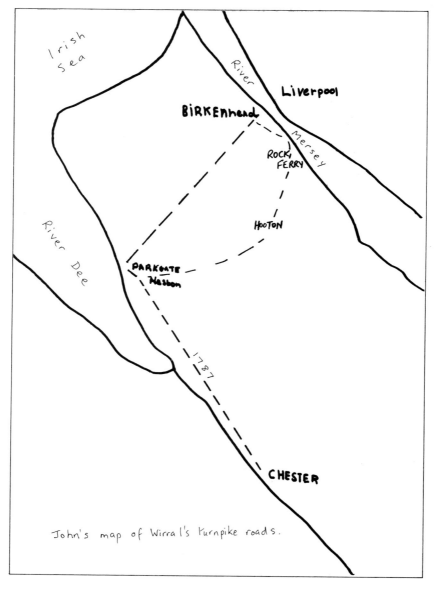

John drew this map to show the turnpike roads

Passengers travelling on turnpike roads paid tolls which helped towards the repair of these roads. John found this copy of the tolls for the Neston-Chester turnpike.

WOODBANK GATE	
Tolls payable at this Gate.	
For every horse, ass, beast or other cattle. Drawing any coach, carriage, chaise, gig or such like carriage, the sum of	6d.
For every Horse drawing any stage coach	4½d.
For every Horse, Ass, Mule or other beast or cattle drawing any wagon, cart, or other such carriage if the wheels are of the breadth of 6 inches or upwards	9d.
If the wheels are of less than 6 inches breadth	6d.
For every Horse, ass or Mule, laden or unladen	2d.
For every Ox, Cow or Meat cattle	½d.
For every Calf, Sheep, Pig or Lamb	¼d.
Alfred Carrin ....Clerk.	
Harvey ....Surveyor.	
Tickets given at this gate to free Shotwick and Badger's Rake side gates.	

In *Pigot's Directory*, 1822, John discovered that horsedrawn coaches ran between Neston cum Parkgate and Liverpool with their timetable 'regulated by the tide at the Flint and Bagilt ferryhouse, Parkgate.'

27

In this extract from *White's Directory*, 1860, John discovered that a new type of vehicle was now being used to carry people. What was it called? Follow its route on John's map. How was it different to earlier types of transport using the turnpike roads? Find a picture of one to make your own drawing.

> Thomas Johnson's ombinus leaves the Boat House twice a day during the summer season for Hooton Station, and for Rock Ferry every Tuesday and Saturday, calling at the Golden Lion Inn, Great Neston.
>
> If the contemplated improvements in the Dee navigation should be completed, and the branch railway to the Chester and Birkenhead line from Hooton to Great Neston be constructed, it is probable this place may gain its former importance. There is a communication with the Welsh coast by ferry-boats.

Having already traced the road and sea history of Neston, John was keen to discover when the railway line was opened. The earliest reference he could find was the one shown above, dated 1860, from *White's Directory*. The line was obviously opened soon after this, because *Morris's Directory*, 1874, (see below), proves that there was a station in use at Neston. From the extract find the evidence that John spotted which shows this. Make a list of all the clues that you find.

Trades and Professions

Adams George, painter, Parkgate Road
Anyon Miles, shoemaker, Parkgate Road
Anyon Samuel, blacksmith, Bridge Street
Anyon Thomas, coal merchant, Neston Station; Brook Street
Ashbrook William, farmer, Bridge Street
Bell Samuel, tailor, The Cross
Bennett William, earthenware dealer, The Cross
Birch Jonathan, tailor, Bridge Street
Boddington Mrs. Louisa Mary, milliner and dressmaker, High Street
Boddington Thomas, professional waiter, High Street
Briscoe William Davies, butcher, High Street
Broster Thomas, carrier, Brook Street
"Brown Horse" inn, The Cross
Cottrell Mrs. Ellen, shopkeeper, Parkgate Road
Cottrell Thomas, grocer and provision dealer, Liverpool Road
Cottrell William, corn dealer, grocer, baker, flour and provision merchant, The Cross
Coventry Richard and John, plumbers, glaziers, tinmen and braziers, High Street
Coventry John (firm of Richard and John Coventry); Parkgate Road
Coventry William, parish clerk, High Street
Crimes William, "White Hart" inn, The Cross
Currie Alexander, grocer and provision dealer, The Cross
Davies Thomas, wheelwright, High Street
Drury Harry William, stationer and smallware dealer, Parkgate Road
Evans Mrs. Catherine, blacksmith and ironmonger, Cross Street
Field Thomas, coal and lime merchant, Neston Station; Liverpool Road
Finney John, beer retailer, Five Lane Ends
Fore Thomas and Co., chemists and druggists and at Birkenhead—Nathaniel James Lewis, manager
Foster William, woollen and linen draper, hatter and hosier, High Street
Garner John, tailor, Cross Street
Gibbons Mrs. Ann, farmer, Upland House
Gibbons John, farmer, Yew Tree House
Gray Wolton, thrashing machine owner, High Street
Griffiths Joseph, boot and shoemaker, Parkgate Road
Grocott William, joiner, builder and contractor, High Street
Hall George, "Brewers' Arms" inn and joiner, High Street
Hancock William, "Golden Lion" commercial inn and livery stable keeper, High Street
Handley Peter, ironmonger and whitesmith, Liverpool Road
Hartley Miss Ellen, Berlin wool and fancy repository, High Street
Henshaw George, boot and shoemaker, Parkgate Road
Hobley Henry, grocer, provision dealer and insurance agent, Park Street
Hodgson James, chemist and druggist, High Street
Hodgson Miss Sarah, postmistress, High Street
Huddart Jacob, market gardener, Rose Cottage, Five Lane Ends
Hughes Henry, stationmaster
Hughes William, "Plough" inn, Park Street
Hynes Francis, sergeant drill instructor, Burton Road

28

Above is an old photo of Neston South Station which opened in 1866.

Use your local Directories to find out how the road and rail links developed where you live. Turnpike roads began to be popular in the eighteenth century (more than 250 years ago) and railways around the middle of the nineteenth century (over a hundred years ago).

Changing trades

Inns

While looking through *Pigot's Commercial Directory* of 1822, John was surprised to find so many inns and public houses listed for the small village of Neston cum Parkgate.

> *Inns and Public Houses.*
> Barrel, John Bethell, *Parkgate*
> Black Bull, Elizabeth Bellin
> Blue Bell, Daniel Oakea
> Brewer's Arms, Wm. Matthews
> Coach and Horses, Jonathan Davies
> Flint and Bagillt Ferry-house, Geo. Barlow, *Parkgate*
> Golden Lion, John Roberts
> Greenland Fishery, Martha Guile
> Mostyn Arms Inn, Esther Briscoe, *Parkgate*
> Nag's Head, James Norman
> Plough, John Smith
> Princess Royal, Joseph Gibbons
> Princess Royal, John Williams, *Parkgate*
> Red Lion, John Wood, *Parkgate*
> Sawyers Arms, Richard Bartley, *Parkgate*
> White Horse, Joseph Davies

John took a photograph of the Red Lion public house, one of the five listed in *Pigot's Directory* that he could find.

This description of Parkgate in *Robson's Commercial Directory* of 1841 gave John a clue to the reason for this large number of inns. Can you spot the clue? Why did most of the inns close?

> Park-gate, or the *New Quay*, is a convenient and fashionable watering place, in the parish of Neston and hundred of Wirrall. It was once celebrated as the station for some of the packets for Ireland, but at present is much neglected as a port, vessels of burthen being prevented from approaching the quay, owing to the formation of a large sand-bank which obstructs the channel. It consists principally of one long and irregular range of houses built of brick, which front the estuary of the Dee, over which is a commodious ferry to Flint. It is 12 miles from Chester and 192 from London.

This old photograph shows The George inn, which later became the Mostyn Arms hotel.

In 1855, the Mostyn Arms became Mostyn House private school. The frontage was altered to its present-day black and white in 1932.

From the Directory list on the opposite page find who was the landlady of the Mostyn Arms in 1822. Who was the landlord of the Red Lion? Look back at pages 11 and 12 to find photograph clues to the other five remaining inns. Make a list of them, noting the names of their landlords.

Tradesnames

This extract from *Kelly's Directory* gives a list of the tradespeople in Neston in 1857.

GREAT NESTON		
Anyon Miles, shoemaker	Gleaves James, beer retailer	Jones Robert, butcher
Ashbrook John, farmer	Guile Ann (Miss), ladies' school	Jones Robert, shopkeeper
Baxter Charles, joiner	Guile Martha. (Mrs.), *Greenland Fishery*	Jones Thomas, farmer
Birch Jonathan, tailor	Hale Richard, miller	Jones Thomas, postmaster
Birks Thomas, boarding school for young gentlemen	Hall George, carpenter	Jones Thomas, saddler
Braid James, surgeon, M.D.	Hall George, *Plough*	Jones William, farmer, Brook Street
Briscoe William, butcher	Handley William, whitesmith	Kenny Elizabeth (Mrs.), baker
Broster Joseph, *Brown Horse*	Hayes Esther (Miss), shopkeeper	Lea Peter, master of National school
Cottrell David, farmer	Heath Jane (Mrs.), shopkeeper	Lloyd John, saddler & harness maker
Coventry William, tinman & brazier, & parish clerk	Henshaw George, earthenware dealer	Lloyd Thomas, currier & fellmonger
Davies Joseph, wheelwright	Hobley Henry, boys' school	McCall Ann (Mrs.), grocer
Davies Thomas, wheelwright	Hodgson James, chemist & druggist	Mackay John, linen & woollen draper
Evans John, blacksmith	Hughes William, farmer	Maddox Jonathan, baker
Evans Robert, blacksmith	Jones & Son, auctioneers, appraisers & general commission agents, & agents to the Liverpool & London fire & life assurance company	Maddox Thomas, baker
Garner John, tailor		Mallinson Emanuel, grocer, tallow-chandler & farmer
Gibson David, watchmaker	Jones Joseph, butcher	Matthews Robert, cooper
		May Francis, joiner
		Mealor John, *Black Bull*
		Mealor John, farmer

John found many of the tradesnames strange, so he looked them up in a dictionary. Which ones would you need to look up? Which of the trades no longer exist? Why? Some are still continued, but have different names. List them, with their modern names.

Here are some sketches of the tradespeople listed in the 1857 Directory. Identify the trades and list the names of the people doing each of these jobs, from the Directory.

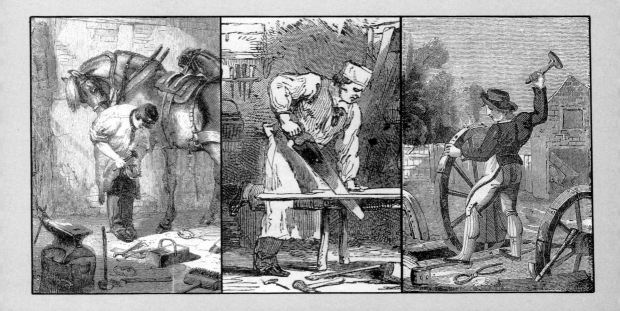

Changing times

Local government

This passage, which John found in *Pigot's Directory*, 1822, describes the meetings of the regional courts for Neston.

> ...The Hundred or Wapentake Court and Court Leet for Wirrall are held at the office of Messrs. Williams and Noble. J. Williams is also Lord Paramount of the hundred, by grant from the Crown, and consequently is entitled to all wrecks, &c. &c. within the Hundred...

John was puzzled by the words *Wapentake* and *Leet* in the description. He found their meanings in a dictionary. You find out what they mean.

A meeting of a regional court in the mid nineteenth century

John found evidence in *Kelly's Cheshire Directory*, 1857, that these local courts were held until 1857.

> The magistrates' sittings are held at the Court House, Great Neston. The Board of Guardians meets at Clatteridge and Birkenhead every Wednesday, alternately. The district is attached to the County Court at Birkenhead. A court leet and court baron are held annually.

However, in 1858, a Local Government Act took this power from the Lord of the Manor. It gave ordinary citizens the chance to sit on local councils and control their own towns as public servants.

By 1902, the *Kelly Directory* showed that Neston cum Parkgate had its own Urban District Council.

NESTON & PARKGATE URBAN DISTRICT COUNCIL

Meets at Town Hall on first Monday in each month, at 7.45 p.m.

Members.
Chairman, Joseph Pemberton.
Vice-Chairman, John Caleb Lloyd

Leighton & Parkgate Ward.

Retire April	Retire April
William Edward Whinnerary 1903	William Jones 1904
	Thomas James Gleave 1905

Neston Ward

Retire April	Retire April
William Gray 1903	John Caleb Lloyd 1904
John Brown Yeoman ...1903	Henry Thomas Gill 1905
Joseph Conway 1904	James Platt 1905

Little Neston Ward

Retire April	Retire April
Joseph Pemberton 1903	William Pritchard 1905
John Woodward 1904	

Officials.
Law Clerk, John Percival Gamon, Cathedral chambers, St. Werburgh street, Chester
Treasurer, Richard L. Price, North & South Wales Bank, Town Hall buildings, High street
Medical Officer of Health, George Arthur Kenyon M.B. Flookersbrook, Chester
Surveyor, Sanitary Inspector & Water Works Manager, Charles Senior, Town hall
Collector, William Tranter, Neston

PUBLIC ESTABLISHMENTS
Free Library, Town hall, John Riddock Ph.D., M.A. hon. librarian
Liberal Club, Hinderton road
Police Station, Sergt. Dick Wharam, in charge, & 3 constables
Town Hall, High street, John George Lee, sec.
Volunteer Fire Brigade, High street

PUBLIC OFFICERS
Collector of Income Taxes, Hugh Coventry, High street
Medical Officer & Public Vaccinator, Neston District, Wirral Union, John B. Yeoman M.D., F.R.C.S.Edin. Parkgate road; deputy, Lewis Grant M.A., M.B.Edin. Parkgate
Registrar of Births, Deaths & Marriages & Vaccination Officer, Neston Sub-District, Wirral Union & Assistant Overseer for Great Neston & Leighton, Edward Kerns, Parkgate road
Assistant Overseer, Little Neston Ward, James Wright Mealor
National School (mixed & infants), built in 1860, for 300 mixed children & 120 infants; average attendance, 244 mixed, 80 infants; Miss Annie Fairbrother, head mistress; Miss Margaret E. Montgomery, infants' mist.
Railway Station, Edwin Rooke, station master
Neston & Parkgate Station (North Wales & Liverpool Railway), Frank Herbert Waite, station master

Carriers
Richard Norton Heath, to Birkenhead & Liverpool, every tues & fri.; George Roberts, to Birkenhead, every sat.

Look at the list of local councillors. Which ones needed to stand for re-election in 1903?

Which public office did John B. Yeoman hold in 1902?

Who was the registrar of births, deaths and marriages?

What was Miss Annie Fairbrother's profession?

Who was in charge of the police station, and how many constables did he have?

Spot the clue which tells you the difference between the fire brigade then and now.

Other changes

John found lots of Directory clues to how life had changed in Neston by the 1930 s. *Kelly's Cheshire Directory* for 1939 contained several clues which suggested that new housing was being built and sold in the town. List any evidence for this that you can find.

COMMERCIAL
Andrew Wm. Cullen D.S.O., M.C., M.B., Ch.B.Glas. physcn. & surgn. (firm, Stewart & Andrew), The Gables, Hinderton rd. T N 121
Anyon Nancy (Miss), dressmkr. Sunnymead, Burton rd
Anyon Thos. bldr. Sunnymead, Burton rd
Appleton's (R. R. Minton & Co. (1930) Ltd.), chandlers, High st. T N 71
Archer Nancy (Miss), teacher of music, Berwyn, Hinderton rd
Ashbrook Geo. farmer
Ashton Jsph. Wm. shopkpr. High st
Askey Albt. dairyman, Mellock farm, Lees la. T N 311
Atkinson Jsph. pastrycook, High st
Baddeley Rd confctnr. Chester rd
Baines Annie Mrs. draper, High st
Baines Rosa (Mrs.), certified midwife, Mayfield gdns
Ball W. T. manager Midland Bank Ltd. & treas. to Urban District Council, Town Hall blds. High st. T N 72
Beattie Emanuel, boot repr. Park st
Benson J. & Son, nurserymen, The Runnell, Leighton. T N 346
Benson Ernest, fruitr. The Cross, T N's 205 & 206
Benyon Sidney, insur. agt. 6 Raby ter. Raby rd
Birch Elizabeth (Mrs.), greengrocer, Bridge street
Bostock Thos. insur. agt. Parville, Raby rd
Bowcock Stanley, market gardener, Windy Ridge, Upper Raby rd. T N 423
Bradleys (Chester) Ltd. clothiers & outfitters, The Cross
Brassey Kate (Mrs.), confctnr. Chester rd
Brazenell Clement Wm. turf commission agt. High st. T N's 504 & 505
Brewers' Arms P.H. (Mrs. Mary Jane McLeavy), Park st
Bridson R. & Son, thrashing machine owners & public works, road & tar spraying contractors, Bridge street. T A "Bridson, Neston;" T N 134
British & Argentine Meat Co. Ltd. High street

Brown Horse P.H. (Regnld. C. Stephens), High st
Buglass Harold B. shopkpr. Chester rd
Burden Harold, nurseryman, The Runnell, Leighton
Burkey Beatrice (Mrs.) ladies' hairdresser, High st. T N 548
Cameron M. C. & Sons, cycle dealers & wireless & motor engineers, The Cross. T N 284
Cannon Margt. (Mrs.), shopkpr. Little Neston
Carlisle, Gunn, Selby & Turner, physicians & surgns. Parkgate rd. T N 58
Carlisle Hy. Geo. M.D., Ch.B. Edin. (firm, Carlisle, Gunn, Selby & Turner), physcn. & surgn. Parkgate rd. T N 58
Carrigan Rt. Wm. market gardener, Moorside ho. Parkgate rd. T N 49
Cartwright Claude Hy. hairdrssr. Bridge st
Cemetery (Arth. Tillotson, supt)
Cheshire Trade Protection & Estate Agency (C. W. Roberts Ltd.), High street. T N 294
Chester Co-operative Society Ltd. High st. T N 86
Chrimes Herbt. hardware dlr. Brook st
Chrimes Jack, haulage contrctr. Olive rd. & Brook st. T N 313
Chrimes Kathln. (Miss), tallow chandler, 1 Hinderton rd
Chrimes Wm. firewood dlr. Brook st
Coach & Horses P.H. (Albt. Marr, Bridge st
Connelly Jas. fried fish dlr. Liverpool rd
Corkill John Robert, hair dresser, High street
Cottrell Mary E. (Mrs.), midwife, Burton rd
Coventry W. M. & Sons, decrtrs. Burton rd
Croxton Thomas, farmer, Leighton rd
Davies Elsie (Mrs.), ladies' hairdrssr. Bridge st. T N 546
Dee Side Riding School, (W. E. Ellison, proprietor), High street, T N 371
Dodd Jn. farmer, Rocklands, Bull hill
Dodd Wltr. farmer, Rose farm, Little Neston
Domino (The) Wine & Spirit Stores (W. A. Howgate, proprietor), The Cross

Douglas Evangeline I. (Miss), district nurse, Raby rd. T N 537
Ellison W. E. see Dee Side Riding School
Ellison Wm. market gardener, Brook st
Evans Jn. boot repr. Bridge st
Evans Rt. chemist, see Kennedy & Evans
Evans Wm. baker, Liverpool rd T N 132
Fairclough Herbt. hairdrssr. High st
Fleming William & Co. builders & contractors, Cross street & Liverpool road T N's 248 & 249
Fleming Albt. bldr. Fairholme, Leighton rd. T N 252
Fogg Thos. tea rms. Liverpool rd. T N 333
Free Library (Miss D. W. Taylor, sec & librarian), Parkgate rd
Friend Elias, farm bailiff to R. Whineray esq. Backwood Hall frm
Gerrard Marion (Mrs.), shopkpr. Liverpool rd
Gilmore Bros. motor engnrs. Leighton garage
Gittins Jsph S. upholsterer, Parkgate rd. T N 126
Gray Charles Ltd. thrashing machine owner, timber merchant mortar grinder & saw mills, Mill house, Leighton road. T N 67
Green Emily (Miss) shopkpr. Little Neston
Green Herbt. Jn. bird food dlr. Bridge st
Greenland Fishery P.H. (Andrew Regnld. Coyle), Parkgate rd
Griffiths Arth. newsagt. Little Neston
Griffiths Geo. boot ma. Bridge street
Gunn George M.B.E., M.D., Ch.B., F.R.C.S.Edin. physcn. & surgn (firm Carlisle, Gunn, Selby & Turner), & assistant physcn. to the Royal Liverpool Country Branch Hospital for Children (Heswall) & public vaccinator to the Urban District Council, Parkgate rd. T N 58
Hale Alred Geo. confr. Parkgate rd
Hall J. & E. (Misses), pastrycooks Parkgate rd. T N 235
Harbrew E. M. relieving officer, Parkgate rd. T N 79
Harp P.H. (Chas. Palfreyman)
Hill Rd. motor engnr. Chester rd T N's 70 & 9

What entry in the Directory suggests that more people were able to read at this time?

35

Which services were available in 1939 which suggest that the people of Neston were becoming more prosperous?

How many of the people listed looked after the health of the people of Neston? Mary Cottrell was one of these. What was her job?

Why do you think the blacksmiths and wheelwrights have gone? Find and list the clues to the new methods of transport.

Local Industry

During his searchings in the local library, John came across this photo. He was surprised to find that there had been coal mining in the area. He decided to see what evidence he could discover about this former local industry.

A group of miners make their way home after the shift in the 1930s

He found this reference in *Bagshaw's Cheshire Directory* of 1850

> At Neston Little are extensive collieries of Mr. Thomas Cottingham, from which extensive quantities of coal were formerly exported to Ireland. The river Dee, however, having become choked up with sandbanks, has completedly stopped traffic.

However, although this 1850 reference suggested that the mine had closed, John discovered that it had re-opened. In *Kelly's Cheshire Directory*, 1892, there is an entry for:

> Wirral Colliery Co. Ltd, agent and secretary Joseph Williams, Manager James Platt.

John sketched a copy of an 1899 local map showing the site of the colliery. Look at the first reference. Spot the clue on John's map which suggests why the mine was re-opened.

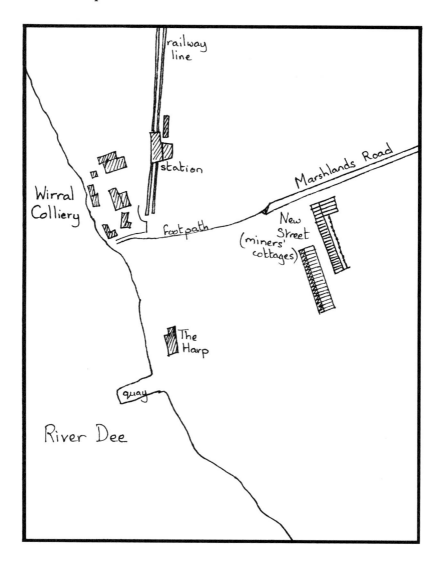

Look closely at John's sketch of the 1899 map (opposite). Can you spot the Harp Inn? This was used by the local *colliers*. John found this old photograph of the Harp at that time.

The *Kelly's Directory*, 1912 reference told John that the colliers were housed by Thomas Cottingham, the owner of the mine, in terrace cottages, built in New Street and Seven Row, behind the Harp. Spot them on John's map.

	NEW STREET		NEW STREET
1	Jones A. miner	2	Williams W. miner
3	Parry D. miner	4	Campin J. miner
5	Burkey J. miner	6	Collins K. labourer
7	Peters J. fisherman	8	Williams R. miner
9	Jones J. miner	10	Smythe I. labourer
11	Gray C. farmworker	12	Flint R. shoe repairer
13	Millington J. miner		
	here is Seven row	14	Williams H. miner
15	Williams J.M. miner	16	Poole A. hairdresser
17	O'Brien P. labourer	18	Thompson M. farmworker
19	Johnson M. miner	20	Robinson T. fisherman

John went out with his camera to discover for himself what evidence remained of the old mining industry at Neston.

The Harp inn today

The Old Quay at Denhall

New Street today

Use your local Directories in the library to collect evidence of any industries in your town which have died out. Like John, you may be able to sketch or photograph any clues to the industrial past which still remain.

History of a street

What do you know about the history of your street? Old Street Directories can give us lots of clues to a street's past. Let us look at a small section of one from 1910.

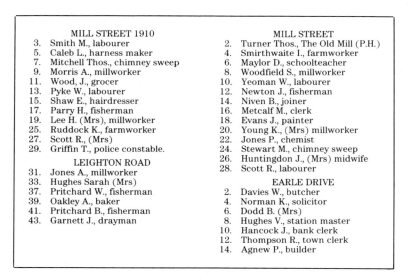

```
        MILL STREET 1910                          MILL STREET
 3.  Smith M., labourer              2.  Turner Thos., The Old Mill (P.H.)
 5.  Caleb L., harness maker         4.  Smirthwaite I., farmworker
 7.  Mitchell Thos., chimney sweep   6.  Maylor D., schoolteacher
 9.  Morris A., millworker           8.  Woodfield S., millworker
11.  Wood, J., grocer               10.  Yeoman W., labourer
13.  Pyke W., labourer              12.  Newton J., fisherman
15.  Shaw E., hairdresser           14.  Niven B., joiner
17.  Parry H., fisherman            16.  Metcalf M., clerk
19.  Lee H. (Mrs), millworker       18.  Evans J., painter
25.  Ruddock K., farmworker         20.  Young K., (Mrs) millworker
27.  Scott R., (Mrs)                22.  Jones P., chemist
29.  Griffin T., police constable.  24.  Stewart M., chimney sweep
                                    26.  Huntingdon J., (Mrs) midwife
        LEIGHTON ROAD               28.  Scott R., labourer
31.  Jones A., millworker
33.  Hughes Sarah (Mrs)                     EARLE DRIVE
37.  Pritchard W., fisherman         2.  Davies W., butcher
39.  Oakley A., baker                4.  Norman K., solicitor
41.  Pritchard B., fisherman         6.  Dodd B. (Mrs)
43.  Garnett J., drayman             8.  Hughes V., station master
                                    10.  Hancock J., bank clerk
                                    12.  Thompson R., town clerk
                                    14.  Agnew P., builder
```

What are the three pieces of information that the Street Directory gives about most houses? Why is there less information about some houses, like 27 Mill Street? A local fisherman and his son live in the same street. What are their addresses? Using the Directory information, list the types of work that go on in the town.

This photograph is a clue to how one of the streets above got its name. Can you guess which street? Name the people in this street whose work links them to the photograph.

41

Look carefully at the extract from the 1910 Street Directory. Who lived at 39 Leighton Road, and what was his job? Draw a sketch showing him at work. Where did the harness maker live? Draw a sketch of him working.

The following photographs show various occupations listed in the 1910 Street Directory. Look at the Directory and work out what they are.

The sketch plan below of the area recorded in the 1910 Directory tells us when the different houses were built. Which is the oldest street? Write down the numbers of the earliest houses that were built. How old are the houses built in Earle Drive? In the Street Directory numbers 21 and 23 Mill Street are not listed. Find the reason by looking at the sketch plan.

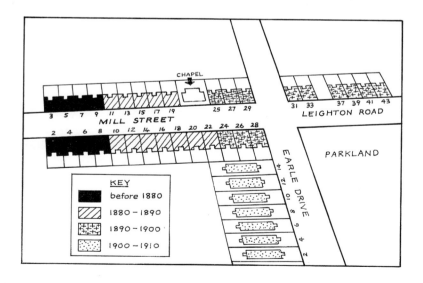

Make a similar plan of your street. Use a *key* to show when the houses were built.

John's grandfather lives in a bungalow in Bull Hill, Little Neston. He showed John this old photograph of the Bull and Dog inn, which once stood at the top of the hill.

Find the correct name for the vehicle standing outside the inn. What was it used for? What would replace it today?

This modern photograph of Bull Hill shows that the Inn buildings remain, but they have changed their use. Can you tell from the photograph how they are used today? Compare the two photographs and find which building has been knocked down.

John found the Bull Inn mentioned in the *Kelly's Directory*, 1906. Find the name of the landlord.

> Riddock John M.A., Ph.D. priv. schl
> Roberts Matthew, Bull inn
> Royden Joseph, farmer
> Scott Robert, farmer
> Smith Joseph, baker & grocer
> Taylor Martha (Mrs.), shopkeeper
> Tickle Thomas, commercial traveller
> Williams Edward, farmer
> Wirral Colliery Co. Lim. (Jas. Platt, manager)
> Woodfield Frederick, shopkeeper & wheelwright

Why do you think the road surface on Bull Hill was in such bad condition. (Clue: note the name of the hill!)

Street names

As John read this extract from *Kelly's Cheshire Directory*, 1906, he noticed that some of the street names gave a clue to the past, because they told him more about the town of Neston.

GREAT NESTON

PRIVATE RESIDENTS.

Bushell Miss, Craig side, Hinderton rd
Chambres William, The Cross
Churton Mrs. Manor house, Moor side
Cottrell Thomas, Liverpool road
Daly Miss, Fair view, Hinderton rd
Fleming Mrs. High street
Foster Miss, Barn acre, Raby road
Frost Samuel Frederick, Highfield
Gamon William, Hinderton road
Glynn Joseph Bird, Moor side
Graham Rev. Harold Jas. M. A. (curate)
Gray Joseph, Mill house
Gray William Ariel, Park view
Hancock Mrs. Church road
Lyon Misses, Elmleigh
McCubbin William A. May cottage
McNeile Rev. George M. A. The Priory
Mansfield Walter, Rose lea, Hinderton road
Mead Wm. Daniel, Yew Tree house
Melynex Thomas, Ambleside, Hinderton road

COMMERCIAL

Anderson J. L. D. S. Edin. dentist, High st. (attends thursdays, 3 to 5 p.m)
Anderson Jn. master mariner, Mex ho
Anyon Miles, jun., shopkeeper, Parkgate road
Badrock Ernest, hardware dealer, High st. & shoeing smith, Brook street
Barraclough Earl, fent dealer, High st
Bell Christian (Miss), district nurse, Brook cottage
Billington J. H. Limited, coal, coke & lime merchants, New Station yd
Billington J. H. & Son, coal merchants, New Station yard
Birch James, tailor, High street
Birch John, insurance agent, High st
Birch Margaret Ethel (Miss, confectioner, High street)
Bradleys (Sidney Clark, managing partner), clothiers & outfitters
Bridson R. & Son, thrashing machine owners & heavy haulage contractors

Briscoe Emma & Charlotte (Misses), fancy repository, The Cross
Briscoe William Norman, farmer
Byrne John, plumber, Park street
Byrne Mary (Mrs.), shopkpr, Park st
Delamore Joseph & Sons, bakers & provender dealers. High street
Dodd William, gardener to J. S. Harmond-Banner esq. Leighton road
Dutton Brothers, clothiers & jewellers, Bridge street
Ellison William, farmer
Evans Ann (Mrs.), shopkpr. High st

45

Here are picture clues to four streets named in the Directory.

Find a street name from each picture clue. What did the names tell John about Neston's past history? Make a list of any street names in your town which give clues to its past. Make a record of any streets or buildings named after famous people or historical events. This will help you to date parts of your town.

How to do it yourself

In this book, we have seen how John used old Local Directories to find evidence about Neston's past. Local Directories can help you to build up a picture of the history of your town.

Go along to your local library, and make a friend of the librarian. He or she can help you find the Directories you need and to understand the evidence in them. The librarian may also be able to arrange for you to meet other useful contacts, such as local historians and collectors of old photographs, whose help can be invaluable. When you go to other libraries, you should always ask to see the *local collection*, as this is usually where local history material is kept.

The *Public Record Office* is another useful place to visit in the nearest city. This is where all the Directories for the area are kept.

We have looked at a number of topics ranging over quite a wide period of time. There is so much information to be found in local Directories that it might prove to be confusing. It might therefore be best to limit yourselves to a short period of time first, no more than a *decade*.

John enjoyed his search for Neston's past, and found many people willing to help. Don't forget to talk to the older people in your town – they will often remember things in great detail, which will bring the Directory evidence to life. You will find further details on how elderly people's memories can bring history alive in *Thanks for the Memory*, another book in the series.

Have a go, you'll be surprised
at how much you discover about your town
– and you'll enjoy yourselves too!

INDEX

Business Pages   6

charter   18
classification   15
council   34
courts   33

fair   19, 20
fishing   22-25
Friendly Society   20, 21

graph   14

local government   33, 34

market   16, 17

mining   37-39

occupations   13, 42, 43

pictorial evidence   8, 9, 12, 39, 40
Public Record Office   47

railway   28, 29

street names   41, 45, 46

tolls   27
turnpike   26, 27

wards   14

Yellow Pages   5, 6

ACKNOWLEDGEMENTS

The author and publishers wish to thank the following for permission to reproduce material:

BBC Hulton Picture Library   pp 32 (middle), 33, 42 (bottom)
Bob Bird   pp 8, 11 (× 4), 16, 22 (× 2), 30, 31 (bottom), 39 (bottom), 40 (× 2), 41, 44 (bottom)
Ian and Marilyn Boumphrey   pp 9, 12, 21, 23, 27, 29, 31 (top), 37, 42 (top), 44 (top)
British Telecom   pp 5, 6
Cheshire County Council Libraries and Museums Department   pp 4, 7
Mansell Collection   pp 32 (left and right), 43
Photo Source   p 19
University College of North Wales   p 18
Derek and Marian Young   pp 19, 39 (top)

Artwork by Clyde Pearson p 15, Steve Cook p 46

Thanks for help in researching this book are recorded to Jenny Archer (Neston Librarian), Chester Record Office and Trudy Boyle.

Cover design by David Armitage

Designed by Bob Wright